Music Minus One Trombone
also playable by Euphonium
and Trombone with F attachment

MOSTLY MOZART
∞ Opera Arias with Orchestra ∞

T0056098

MMO

3996

MOSTLY MOZART
Opera Arias with Orchestra

CONTENTS

Music Minus One
50 Executive Boulevard • Elmsford, New York 10523-1325
914-592-1188 • e-mail: info@musicminusone.com
www.musicminusone.com

SoloTrombone

Der Vogelfänger bin ich ja

from *The Magic Flute*

W.A. Mozart
Edited by Alan Kaplan

Solo Trombone

O Isis und Osiris

from *The Magic Flute*

W.A. Mozart
Edited by Alan Kaplan

MMO 3996

SoloTrombone

Voi, che sapete che cosa e amor

from *The Marriage of Figaro*

W.A. Mozart
Edited by Alan Kaplan

MMO 3996

Solo Trombone

Tardi s'avvede d'un Tradimento

from *La Clemenza di Tito*

W.A.Mozart
Edited by Alan Kaplan

Solo Trombone

Smanie Implacabili
from *Cosi fan Tutte*

W.A. Mozart
Edited by Alan Kaplan

MMO 3996

Smanie Implacabili

Solo Trombone

Fin ch'han dal vino
from *Don Giovanni*

W.A.Mozart
Edited by Alan Kaplan

10

Fin ch'han dal vino

MMO 3996

Solo Trombone

Deh vieni alla finestra

from *Don Giovanni*

W.A.Mozart
Edited by Alan Kaplan

MMO 3996

SoloTrombone

No, la morte io non pavento

from *Idomeneo*

W.A. Mozart
Edited by Alan Kaplan

No, la morte

14

Solo Trombone

Sciocco... qual piacer
from *L'Italiana in Algeri*

Gioacchino Rossini
Edited by Alan Kaplan

Solo Trombone

Ave Maria
from Ellens Gesang III

Franz Schubert
Edited by Alan Kaplan

All transcriptions by Kevin Mauldin

Music Minus One
914-592-1188 • www.musicminusone.com

ISBN 978-1-941566-74-9